In That Secret Place

An Abortion Survivor's Story

Terri Kellogg
Hope Hoffman

"Before I formed you in the womb I knew you..."
~ Jeremiah 1:5

www.xulonpress.com

~ I dedicate this book to Tonya, Hope's birthmother. You gave the most precious gift anyone could give. I am forever grateful. ~

TABLE OF CONTENTS

Introduction

My adopted daughter, Hope, survived an abortion in the first trimester. She continued to grow in that secret place, the womb. Hope's story is about God's perfect timing, grace and forgiveness.

In *In that Secret Place* you will hear two distinct voices: the adoptive mother's and Hope's, an abortion survivor who lives with a disability as a result. You will view life's journey through the eyes of a child who has faced death, trials and tribulations with God's hand of protection being sufficient to meet each challenge. You can learn from Hope's story that no life or circumstance is too small for significance. God is not a condemning God. He loves us and wants to give us the desires of our hearts. He is a God of second chances. He is the way maker and no matter what we have done He wants to reconcile.

If you have wondered where your path is leading you or you have tried to understand God's ways, you are not alone. Our journey was filled with unknowing and learning to trust in the "way maker". *In That Secret Place,* God shows us that He is not just at work when we see His hand through answered prayer, but He is right there all the time creating something beautiful of our life through the difficult times. *In That Secret Place* reveals God's plans are bigger and better than what we could ever hope or dream. You will be inspired to do all God has called you specifically to do by stepping out in faith and knowing He will make a way. You will see anew your trials and tribulations as a strengthening of your faith.

If you have secrets that have kept you in shame and condemnation, *In That Secret Place* allows an opportunity for you to understand and experience His ultimate forgiveness. Forgiveness will not just be for someone else. Forgiveness will have new meaning to you as you realize God's love for you, because you are His child.

Terri

I was too young to remember the actual abortion, but I do have the scar on my head from when I was born. My skull and scalp were cut open by the abortion instrument. I don't really like to think about it. I definitely do not want to see anything on the internet about abortion. I heard them talking about abortion on the news one night and I thought they were talking about me. My mom told me, "No honey they are talking about all the babies that have died in abortion." They tell me I am a miracle because I survived an abortion. They call me 'special needs' because I have Cerebral Palsy and I am in a wheelchair. All I know is God has a plan for my life. I like to tell people God has a plan for their life too.

Hope

The Phone Call

"Trust in the Lord with all your heart and lean not on your own understanding. In all your ways acknowledge him, and he will make your paths straight."

~ Proverbs 3:5-6

It was a phone call that would change the rest of my life. As the phone rang on the other end, I was hesitant and did not want to get my hopes up again. The month before, I worked with an adoption agency to adopt two children, but another family was chosen for them. I was still heartbroken over the loss, but I awoke that morning knowing it was time to move out of my pain. Today I was calling a Christian adoption agency, where I had already completed initial paperwork, but wanted to be placed on their waiting list. The adoption caseworker answered the phone and I explained the situation. The receptionist said, "There is a special needs baby girl we are working with who is available for adoption, but she remains in the hospital at this time. Would you like more information?"

I was never really interested in adopting a baby, but I heard myself say, "Sure." I was thinking, *a baby*? Well, why not? It can't hurt to hear about her. I had learned not to get too excited, because nothing was ever a sure thing no matter how much you wanted it. I waited anxiously as the call was transferred to an adoption caseworker. I doodled on a yellow legal pad totally unaware and slightly detached, protecting myself from disappointment. I couldn't help but wonder—*is this the one?*

The caseworker came on the line, and I switched from doodling to jotting down information as she summarized:

- Born August 12, 1991
- Two months premature baby girl
- Weight: three pounds six ounces
- Currently one month old
- Remains in NICU
- Traumatic birth

She paused and caught her breath, then told me the most amazing story I had ever heard. At ten and a half weeks pregnant, the birthmother went to an abortion clinic to abort the baby. But God had other plans, and unbeknownst to the birthmother or the abortionist, the baby survived. This precious infant continued to grow in secret. It wasn't until the birthmother was five and a half months pregnant that she felt movement and realized her baby was still alive! The caseworker said, "She decided to place the baby for adoption and worked with a lawyer toward a private adoption, but everything changed when she delivered two months early. The baby required CPR two times and was placed on a ventilator."

She continued, "The extent of her disability is unknown, but there were large bleeds in her brain causing probable irreversible brain damage. More than likely she has Cerebral Palsy." She went on to explain, "The baby has a large injury to her head as a result of the instrument used in the abortion that was meant to end her life. The skull and scalp were scraped away leaving jagged edges from her forehead back to her right ear exposing her brain. The baby's scalp was repaired surgically after birth, but she will have a large scar where hair will never grow and a pucker on her forehead that could be repaired later."

My thoughts were racing to process all this information as I rushed to make notes. I was afraid to ask, but I had to know, "Is this baby going to live?" I just didn't know if I could take in a baby who was going to die.

The caseworker's tone was upbeat when she said, "She is off the ventilator and has gained weight, although slowly due to her poor sucking reflex. However, she is a fighter! And we believe with therapy and time she will grow stronger and thrive in a loving home. She will need to remain in the hospital for a couple more months."

"Are there other families interested in adopting her?"

"Originally, yes. Prior to her premature birth several families were being considered for adoption through a private lawyer, but have since changed their minds because they wanted a healthy baby. Due to the baby's special needs, her birthmother has placed her with us. She was not available for adoption until today. Her birthmother waited one month and just came in today to sign all the paperwork. You are the first person we have told about this baby."

Though I held back my excitement, I wanted to shout, "I want her!" Instead, I told the social worker, "I'll talk to my husband, Blair, when he gets home from work and I'll get back to you.

Please know that I am very interested in learning more about her."

I thanked her for the information and immediately began to cry as I hung up the phone. I asked aloud: *Is this the child I've waited for? After wanting an older child how can I be excited about a baby? And a girl?* I kept mulling over the information. I was excited, but for some reason I felt hesitant to the idea. *God is this You? Or is this me feeling desperate?* I didn't want to go through the pain of losing another child.

While I didn't realize it, God was in preparation mode. I had been asking Him to prepare us for the child He had for us. Though I had never wanted a baby, my feelings had changed over the last nine months. I had never imagined it would happen this way, but I was sure God knew exactly what He was doing.

Journal excerpts written after another family was chosen for the two children we were seeking to adopt.

July 11, 1991

I haven't done much of anything over the last couple weeks. I cry and don't give of myself to anyone. It's difficult to reach out and care for anyone when you feel crushed and deeply disappointed. Just the thought of the children brings tears. I can't understand it. The feelings are so deep. I'm not motivated to do anything but meet my own needs. I don't want to cry anymore because it hurts too much. I said out loud to someone the other day, "I still love God even though He didn't give us the children, so He will still love me even though I'm not reading my Bible." With those words I felt relief, not the kind of guilt I usually felt from neglecting quiet time with God. I've never felt this way before. Not rebellious—just kind of indifferent.

I never realized it, but I've become accustomed to getting what I want when I want it. Having never been so deeply disappointed before, I now know how it feels, and the pain is so intense it's hard to describe. I haven't turned my back on God. I have no doubt He is working to prepare us for His will. I can believe nothing else. Lord, what are we to do?

A Mother's Grief

By Terri

How do you feel the loss of what you've never had?

How can that which was never yours be taken

away?

A death of a vision makes me sad.

There's an emptiness that won't go away.

A vision so real and even confirmed by a dream.

Signs of encouragement give hope

My heart aches with the remembrance

of what seemed mine, is now another's.

July 23. 1991

Sometimes I don't know if I am growing, standing still or moving backward. This past month I've felt extremely sad and empty. A couple of days ago at work a patient's family member showed me a picture of Jesus, and the woman said, "I hope you know Him." I realized it was apparent that I had lost my joy.

My heart still hopes for the children. August 12th is nine months exactly from the date we first met the children. It seems as though my heart refuses to cut the emotional ties with them until then.

~~~~~~~~~~~~~~~~~~~~~

On August 12, 1991 a miracle baby girl was born. She had been fighting desperately for her life since the day her birthmother entered the abortion office. A month later our paths were crossing...with the phone call that changed the rest of our lives.

. . . And God Named Her Hope

"Hope deferred makes the heart sick,

but a longing fulfilled is a tree of life."

~ Proverbs 13:12

I always knew I would one day adopt a child. The Lord had planted that desire in my heart as far back as I can remember. I had no desire to go through pregnancy and delivery. In fact, I wanted to skip the baby stage entirely and adopt an older child because I wasn't really a "baby-person." I had it all figured out; I would marry and we would adopt a little boy about two or three years old when we were ready—maybe even a special needs child.

I always had a heart for special needs children. Throughout my years in high school, I volunteered with the Special Olympics and helped in a special education class. I had even planned to attain a degree in Special Education before later changing to a degree in nursing.

So when this precious baby girl met our path, I was partially comfortable with the idea of a special needs child with one small exception ~ she was a baby! It was no surprise to me when my husband did not share in my initial excitement.

It was not exactly what we had agreed upon. We had been married five years and we had prepared ourselves for a child, not a baby.

I asked my husband, "Won't you even consider that this baby may be God's will for us?"

He tilted his head to study my face and responded, "I didn't think you wanted a baby." I could tell from his facial expression that he was surprised and angry at being caught off guard at the suggestion that this could be God's will for us.

With a timid smile I said simply, "I changed my mind."

His reluctance was obvious when he said, "You can continue to get information about the baby, but I'm not saying yes yet. I don't want you to get your hopes up because I'm not hopeful."

The truth was that I wanted this baby, but only if God wanted us to have her. I prayed that if this was God's will He would show Blair. My heart was already captivated by this baby girl and I had not even seen her. I wanted to make sure this was the right child for us, and not just a result of my desperate desire to be a mother. I wanted us to be united in our excitement about our decision.

I told the adoption caseworker that my husband was uncertain, but that he was open to learning more about the baby. The caseworker was as excited as I was, despite my husband's hesitation. I talked to the agency almost every day and jotted down note after note about this baby girl. Though I dared not read too much into it, it appeared that God was at work. I already knew I had given my heart away.

One afternoon I asked the caseworker, "What is the baby's name? I want to know what to call her."

The caseworker explained, "For confidentiality reasons I'm not yet able to give you her name."

Without thinking, I wrote the name "Hope" on a piece of paper. Having never thought of that name before I knew it was from God. That was especially clear after I looked up the original meanings of the word "hope." One special meaning is *something waited for with expectation.*[1]

We had made plans to go on a cruise at the end of September, but a part of me wanted to stay home so I could keep up with this little girl's progress. I had learned by experience that when you're seeking God's will, it doesn't matter how much you want something, He will not give it to you if it is not best for you. I continued to pray that God would lead us and show us His will. Though I was already convinced she was the one for us I didn't want to pressure Blair. I chose to let go of impatience and went on the cruise as we had planned.

While we were on the cruise, God did something amazing. We were placed at a table with three other couples with whom we would eat all our meals for one week. Only God could have ordained that each couple had a close relationship with a special needs child. The couple we spent the most time with had a toddler with Down's Syndrome. We talked late into the night about life with a special needs child. To be honest, what they had to share was not always encouraging. They offered a much needed reality check through candidly sharing their experience.

Another woman at our table said that her brother had Cerebral Palsy. She spoke from the viewpoint of someone who had grown up with a handicapped sibling and how her life had been blessed by his presence in the family. Interestingly enough, the third couple's best friends had just adopted a child with Cerebral Palsy. It was a confirmation to me that this wasn't just my desperate desire to be a mother to any child; this was God clearly working things out in His own time. It was as if God was saying, "I chose this child for you. Don't for one moment think you are choosing her. My ways are not your ways. Remember, you didn't even want a baby." So I can take no credit; it was all God. Even Blair acknowledged this baby girl might be God's will for us.

As I look back at the timing of everything, I can see that while our future daughter was being formed in her mother's womb, God was keeping me preoccupied with the other two adoptive children until the very day of Hope's birth on August 12th! Though for different reasons, both Blair and I needed those nine months for God to prepare our hearts. It was clear to me at this point God knows us better than we know ourselves.

Each day seemed like an eternity as we waited for her to be discharged from the hospital. It was very difficult to know that this fragile little baby girl was out there and we had no ability to see, touch or hold her. We lived one and a half hours north of the adoption agency and were anxious to visit the hospital to see our baby. However, the adoption agency did not believe that was a good idea for us to visit due to the circumstances.

The caseworker told me when I made another request for a visit, "The hospital staff is very attached and protective of her. They want to meet you both in person and approve of you. They are also quite attached to the birthmother because she visits daily." For that reason, the agency thought confidentiality was best for everyone.

Instead of a face-to-face visit, we were given two Polaroid pictures of our soon to be little girl. It was at this point that she became a reality to us. She was very small—a precious miracle of God. The **HOPE** we had waited for.

We had made several requests to learn more about Hope's physical condition, but her doctor refused to talk to us on the phone. Any questions we had regarding Hope's condition or care would have to go through the adoption agency. As a nurse this was very difficult for me. I wanted to hear for myself directly from the doctor the extent of brain damage, her prognosis and her current level of development.

Feeling deeply frustrated when I couldn't get any answers, I took the information I did have and called a local pediatric neurologist. He returned my call as a courtesy and listened as I told him Hope's history and physical condition over the past two and half months.

He quietly responded, "Find another child. There are a lot of children out there. She's too sick, find a healthy one."

I thanked him for taking my call but continued to believe that this was our child. In fact, that conversation brought me once again to the realization that God was in control and only He knew all the answers.

The adoption agency sent a foster mother to the hospital to learn how to care for Hope so she could teach us once the adoption was complete. The foster mother said that every time she went to visit Hope one of the nurses was always holding her. It was clear the nurses were very attached to her and often brought things to decorate and personalize her crib. We were able to communicate

29

with the foster mother on a few occasions. One time the foster mother told me, "You know, I too am falling in love with this baby. If you don't adopt her I will!"

I listened as she told me her story, "I had an abortion when I was younger and I've never completely recovered from it. Until now, I've never been able to forgive myself." I listened compassionately as she continued, "This precious baby has helped me receive God's unconditional love and forgiveness." The message was clear: without a single spoken word God used this little one to mend a broken heart.

The doctor wanted Hope to weigh more than six pounds before she was discharged from the hospital. As we waited for her to gain weight, the foster mother continued to visit Hope, as we prepared for her arrival. We rented how-to videos and read a number of books on caring for babies. After all, we had not been planning on adopting a baby until two months ago. We decorated the nursery and installed new carpet. Both our church and my work gave us baby showers. We were blessed with all the things needed to care for a baby: diapers, bottles, wipes, bibs, bathtub, soaps, clothes and blankets. With every passing day we came closer to being a family.

Journal excerpts:

Sept. 17, 1991

Lord, I pray for this little girl and know Your hand is upon her. Pour out Your love on her when she is alone with no one to hold her. Bring her joy, Lord. Bless her, Lord and heal her body. Keep Your hand upon her and put a sparkle in her eye so that those who see her will know she is a miracle child. No matter what the circumstance or suffering give her HOPE because Your hand is on her. Help her hold onto Your promises, giving her strength to go on when odds are against her.

The words from a special Petra song I remember reflect the peace I felt. . . *This is my prayer lifted to You. Knowing You care even more than I do. This is my prayer lifted in Your name. Your will be done I humbly pray.*

Used by permission

Homecoming

"Every good and perfect gift is from above, coming down from the Father of the heavenly lights, who does not change like shifting shadows."

~ James 1:17

On November 17, 1991, we anxiously drove one and a half hours south to Hollywood, Florida. By then Hope was three months old, weighed six pounds six ounces and had been discharged from the hospital two days earlier. We were going to pick up our little girl; Hope Olivia at the adoption agency. We had an empty car seat in the backseat that would soon hold the center of our universe. The caseworker greeted us as we entered the small older house that housed the adoption agency. She led us toward the back of the building. I could hardly keep from running past her to see my little girl, but resisted the temptation. The sense of anticipation was like nothing I had ever experienced before. As we entered the room, several people were surrounding the little baby girl who had just arrived. As she was being taken out of the car seat by her foster mother we walked closer. We could see that she looked beautiful in a little white and pink floral headband that covered the little pucker on her forehead that remained after the surgery to close her scalp. I didn't see how fragile she looked. All I saw was Hope, the most precious gift I had ever received. She was alert and content as she looked around and sucked on a pacifier that almost covered half of her face.

Blair walked over and, with a Daddy's instinct, immediately lifted her into his arms without hesitation. While I had been waiting for an invitation, he knew just what to do. As he held her close and their eyes met, I knew then she was going to be Daddy's little girl. From that moment on, God's little lamb was placed in our care and all the waiting and heartache seemed worth it. Everyone in the room seemed to disappear as we held her close. We were instantly unable to imagine life without her.

It was amazing how natural it felt to have that little six pounds, six ounces baby girl at the center of our universe. I was so thankful God did not give me what I thought I wanted all my life (older children). God's promises are true, "Delight yourself in the Lord and he will give you the desires of your heart" (Psalms 37:4). He knew much better than I did what I needed. Looking back now I cannot have imagined missing those baby years with my little girl. It didn't matter one bit that we weren't Hope's biological parents. It was already true that we could not have loved her more.

In those first few days at home, we could tell that Hope had received a great deal of love from the hospital staff where she'd spent her first three months of life, because she would cry every time someone put her down. In addition to the love she received, she came home with a small cardboard box filled with things the staff had bought for her.

Through the eyes of a baby:

I have a Minnie mouse doll that the nurses always squeak to get my attention. Minnie's face was always smiling at me in the crib when no one else was there. One of my favorite nurses bought me a little Snoopy sweat suit to wear home to meet my mom and dad for the first time. My birthmother gave me a baby giraffe that moves it head and plays a lullaby. I like to hear it, because it reminds me of her.

He Holds the Future in His Hands

"For I know the plans that I have for you,"
declares the Lord, "plans to prosper you and
not to harm you, plans to give you a hope
and a future."

~Jeremiah 29:11

The first few weeks after we brought Hope home many visitors came to meet our new addition. I surprised everyone as they came to the front door with a surgical mask and hand sanitizer. I wanted to protect my little premature girl from all germs. For the first three months, except for doctors' appointments two or three times a week, we didn't even leave the house. And though my little girl survived an abortion, I feared what would happen if she got sick. Soon, I realized Hope was far more resilient than I initially thought. I was a first-time mother with a heavy dose of paranoia. In time, we began to take Hope everywhere. She loved to be on the go to the mall, the doctor's office, visiting friends, grocery shopping and church.

Our first year together was very busy with more appointments than I had ever imagined. For Hope's first three years I spent the majority of my time taking her to one kind of therapy or another. I was grateful that she enjoyed her time there.

I certainly made many new friends who were going through similar situations. It was a time of therapy for the moms also.

The consensus among therapists and doctors was that Hope did indeed have Cerebral Palsy, the result of a lack of oxygen and brain hemorrhages at birth. While the damaged area of her brain affected the right side of her body more, her left side was still involved. As an infant, Hope would often lay her right palm open on her scar as if she was protecting it. Today her right arm and hand are unable to reach this area.

My body doesn't always do what I want it to do. But I don't give up—I keep trying. I especially like to be cheered on by an audience.

People have always tried to get me to use my right hand. It doesn't cooperate. I only use it when I have to. I can do everything with my left hand now. My mom told me a 'cookie' story. When I was a baby they gave me a cookie in my right hand and I couldn't get it to my mouth. I tried and tried. My left hand tried to help my right hand by pulling it to my mouth. Finally, she told me I got tired and just grabbed the cookie out of my right hand and shoved it in my mouth with my left hand! Sometimes it is too much work.

Hope's little body was very tight and fought hard against natural movement. It was difficult to fight a constant brain impulse that triggered tightness with every movement. Hope's muscles tightened when she talked, laughed, sang and attempted most any activity. Unlike most babies who learn naturally as they develop, Hope required much help. At that time, the extent of her disability was still unknown, which meant we all worked very hard to overcome obstacles and challenges to enable her to function at the highest level possible. Because of her stiff posture she couldn't grab and hold onto you with her arms. Her body didn't respond to normal touch; when held close she remained quite stiff.

My mom told me the first time I hugged her was when I was 14 months. I had been swimming and I was so relaxed that my arms just stretched around her neck, I don't really remember it. My mom, well she remembers it and when she tells me the story I think I remember it too. I hug her now all the time. People tell me I give the best hugs. Sometimes I just don't let go and that's a problem!

When Hope was six months old, we began to notice a new reflex. She began to startle as if she was falling many times during the day. I once counted twenty-five events in one day. I told every doctor and each passed it off as a hyperactive startle reflex. It was not until I videotaped Hope and showed her neurologist what she was doing that he took me seriously. At that time he ordered a 24-hour EEG to monitor her brain activity. The test results showed a short seizure occurred with each episode and Hope was then diagnosed with epilepsy. If not treated, the seizure activity could have interfered with her learning and development. Not surprisingly, seizures are common among children who have CP due to the brain damage. Hope was placed on seizure medication which controlled her seizures.

This diagnosis was a relief, but it brought sadness, too. My mother's intuition had been right, but now my little girl had another diagnosis—epilepsy. I was sad for her and for myself. That was one more thing to make her different from other children and one more thing for me to worry about. Even though it seemed silly at the time, I couldn't help but grieve for her and myself. I realized that grief could not be ignored or denied. It was a process that I knowingly went through.

Throughout her early childhood years, Hope had several febrile seizures (seizures caused by fevers). Even my experience as a nurse had not prepared me for seeing this happen to my little girl. I was so frightened as I watched her body stiffen and her eyes stare off into space. But when her breathing appeared to stop for what seemed like hours was when it really hit me. Having no control over the situation magnified my fears to the point of panic that I would lose her. One particular time when Hope was about five years old and hospitalized following a seizure, I called my mom.

"You need to give Hope to God. Just turn her over to Him. You can't live in fear," Mom said. "I'm going to pray for God to give you peace."

As she prayed, I let go of the fear and panic by knowing that God loved her even more than I did. I found comfort in remembering how He spared her life before she was born. I had to trust Him, there was nothing else I could do. So I was then able to set worry aside and rest.

The following morning Hope woke and said she'd had a dream. It was the first time she had mentioned dreaming except for occasional nightmares which sometimes woke her up crying.

"I was flying," she said.

"I've had that dream before," I replied. "And it was great! I loved that dream."

Hope's eyes widened. "Did you ride on the angel's back, too?"

"No. Did you?"

"Yes!" she shouted, her smile stretched from ear to ear, as her body stiffened with excitement.

I was a little apprehensive as I asked, "What did you do, Hope?"

"We went to heaven and saw Jesus."

Goose bumps covered my arms. Just the night before I wondered how long I would have Hope alive with me. My question remained unanswered and the thought of her going to heaven soon didn't comfort me at all. But she was excited! That picture of Hope riding on an angel's back to heaven and into the arms of Jesus was planted in my heart that morning, giving me something to hold on to when that day comes.

As much as we might not want to believe it, life and death are far out of our control. It's frightening to realize that life can change in a split second, forever changing life as we know it. And when you have a sick child, tomorrow doesn't matter; today is all that matters. You can barely look past one second to the next. God doesn't always answer our prayers the way we would wish for, but we can be confident that He is in control and we can trust Him. *Thank you, Lord for answers to prayers. Even when I don't understand, I will trust in You always.*

Seizures have always been a part of my life. I remember the big ones. I remember going to the hospital in the ambulance, the paramedics smelling like peanut butter. I like being taken care of. Hospitals do not scare me. Having my blood drawn is not a big deal. They use a butterfly needle and I don't even cry. I usually am the one to remind my mom "It's time to get my blood checked again." And she says, "You are right." One year I spent the night in the hospital on Christmas Eve, and Santa brought my presents to my hospital room while I slept.

I take medicine for my seizures even though I don't have big ones anymore. I still have jerking in my arm and head sometimes. I've even thrown my drink and cell phone during these 'jerks'. It feels like I have no control of my body, but rather my body has control over me. The doctor told Mom these new 'jerks' are not seizures, but I think I need another EEG. My mom listens to me and together we try to get to the root of my problems.

Seizures don't scare me, but I am afraid of falling. I fell at school and fractured my femur after I was left alone on the edge of my wheelchair in the bathroom. Another time, my caregiver dropped me and it frightened us both until we cried. I never want her to take care of me again. I forgave her, but I was still angry and didn't feel safe around her. I have fallen many times. My mom and dad want me to be safe so we make sure to train everyone really well to take care of me. I know accidents happen, but I can't forget. When I remember it makes me afraid all over again.

I know God takes care of me. I had a nightmare once and I woke up crying. My mom came running to my room and told me it was a dream. When she left my room I sang a song to make me feel better. When I am afraid I will trust in You and then I fell back to sleep. I try to not be afraid.

Unanswered Prayers

"'My grace is sufficient for you, for my power is made perfect in weakness.' Therefore I will boast all the more gladly about my weaknesses, so that Christ's power may rest on me."

~ 2 Corinthians 12:9

W hen Hope was an infant my mom suggested, "I think you should take Hope to a healing service."

"Mom, we aren't praying for healing. We believe God did heal her. He spared her life."

God spared her life the day of the failed abortion. Out of the 4,380 babies who were aborted daily in the United States during that time,[2] Hope survived. The doctor described the injury to Hope's head in her medical records as "a large scalp and skull trauma having the appearance of an old wound with extra skin pushed to one side." Hope's very life is a miracle.

Hope is one of God's miracles despite the large scar on her head, cerebral palsy, epilepsy, scoliosis and her need for a wheelchair. Through the years we have had complete strangers walk up to us and, with good intentions, ask us, "Are you praying for her healing?"

Now, I believe God is able to do far beyond what I ask. I have seen God answer many specific prayers through the years. Whether it is for a van with a wheelchair lift, a wheelchair friendly home, a lift for the pool, a hot tub for Hope, a lift to transfer her more easily, a vacation, or a caregiver to meet our needs, time and time again God has provided for our every need.

Sometimes prayers were not answered the way I had hoped. Physical healing for Hope was not received and at times I questioned, "Was it my lack of faith from the beginning?" Over the years we tried many therapies and treatments to help with Hope's Cerebral Palsy. We prayed for Hope to walk, but no matter how hard we worked, our little girl was still as stiff as she could be and walking remained very difficult.

For a long time I have been working hard to dress myself. It takes me quite a while to put my shirt on. Today I couldn't find the arm hole and I called for help. At times I get really distracted, and they keep telling me, "Put your shirt on." If I wait long enough they have to do it because we have run out of time and I will be late to school. At times my mom has called me lazy, and that really hurts my feelings. She apologizes and tells me, "I was frustrated." And, of course, I forgive her.

To be honest, I had trouble believing that I couldn't change some of the effects of the Cerebral Palsy on Hope's body if I just worked a little harder. I had unknowingly been carrying burdens that were never mine to carry. As a Christian, I would have told you I trusted in God with my problems, but my actions did not match my words. Jesus said, "Come to me, all you who are weary and burdened, and I will give you rest" (Matthew 11:28). God began a deeper work in my spiritual walk when I was ready to recognize this disobedience in my life.

Trusting in God became more than words to me. I started to learn what "trusting God" looked like in action. I had to evaluate my need to fix people and situations in order to feel secure. I realized part of my daily stress was caused by not accepting Hope for who she was. I had been trying to accomplish the impossible...to do it all, to be it all. But what would this accomplish? It would have resulted in a stressed-out mom and a stressed out child who still had Cerebral Palsy.

Admittedly, I struggled with accepting situations that did not go as planned. I was unwilling to face my own limitations. I had to be taught what was within my realm of responsibility. For example, there were many years, I felt everything was my responsibility. I even believed Hope's spinal curvature, which eventually required surgery, was a result of my failure to prevent it. I learned to let go of many things out of my control and I began to truly trust in God.

Finally, I came to a place of accepting that God created Hope in her birthmother's womb and allowed these things to be part of her life. Acceptance is not always easy for parents, friends, family and even strangers when there is a child with a disability. Then I read in the Bible, Jesus' disciples asked him, "Rabbi, who sinned, this man or his parents, that he was born blind?"

"Neither this man nor his parents sinned," said Jesus, "but this happened so that the works of God might be displayed in him" (John 9:2-3).

Hope glorifies God in her life through the love and joy she freely gives to others. To be content in a body less than perfect speaks volumes. From the beginning of Hope's life, it was obvious who had named her "Hope". She had been drawn to God since birth. She had prayed to accept the Lord the summer of 1997 at Vacation Bible School when she was six years old. One Saturday she was watching a Christian Camp on TV and some children were being baptized. While she was watching she said, "I want to be baptized!" When I asked her why, she raised her hand to the heavens and said, "Because I believe in Jesus!"

There was never any doubt that Hope trusts in God. Clearly God was present with her, holding and comforting her in the womb. It is no wonder she knew His voice and continues to follow Him now.

Even now when the burdens seem heavy, I slow down and look at my little girl's profile. I see that smile and hear her laugh, and it reminds me of how much God loves me. I see the scar on her head, and I am reminded God has brought her through beautifully and He cares more about her than I do. Her future is in His hands and He is more than able to care for all of her needs. This truth comforts me and reminds me not to worry, but encourages me to trust God and pray. It has been a process of learning to let go of those things that are beyond my control. Now the challenges don't seem so insurmountable when placed in their proper perspective.

Spiritual insight:

One night my mom asked, "Hope, is it always easy for you to trust God?"

I said, "Yes!"

"Why?" she asked.

I said, "Because I know God is always with me and He will always take care of me."

My mom asked me, "Why is it hard for me sometimes?"

I said, "Because you need to spend more time with your friend, God. You need to read your Bible more."

When some prayers seem to go unanswered I know God is faithful and He knows better than I. It is easy to praise the Lord in good times, but when we pass through trials and hardship He is ever present, and that is enough. I will say "He has been good to me". I have a favorite song by Scott Krippayne, and I pray that the words to the song could be said of my life.

"If I never get to see another rainbow or share

another laugh with a friend.

If I never stand barefoot by the ocean or get to

kiss my child good night again.

If I never have another prayer that's answered, or

have another blessing come my way.

If this is all I know of heaven's kindness.

Father I would still have to say,

You have been good.

In so many ways You have been good to me.

You have shown me mercy upon mercy.

Grace upon grace, time after time,

And I know all too well what I'm deserving,

Yet You are so patient and kind.

If suddenly it all were ended and Your blessings

disappeared;

Looking back over a lifetime the evidence is

clear. . .

You have been so good to me."

Used by permission

All Life Has Purpose

"For you created my inmost being; you knit me together in my mother's womb. I praise you because I am fearfully and wonderfully made; your works are wonderful, I know that full well. My frame was not hidden from you when I was made in the secret place. When I was woven together in the depths of the earth, your eyes saw my unformed body."

~ Psalm 139:13-16

From the first day I set my eyes on Hope at the adoption agency, I saw LIFE. I saw her frailty, but didn't see her inabilities. I took note of the scar on her head that spanned from her forehead back to her right ear leaving a visible pucker in the middle of her forehead where the scalp was surgically closed at birth. This pucker would later be named "the kissing spot" by Hope as she grew older. It was the perfect place for my lips to form against her forehead where I would kiss her each day. So whenever Hope is asked today, "What is that?" She tells them, "My *kissing spot.*" This spot is a reminder and reassurance of God's mighty protective hand that day He spared her life in that secret place. I did not know what the future held for Hope, but I knew God had a purpose for her life.

In the early years most doctors and therapists were reluctant to give me much hope, mainly to prevent me from having false expectations. They thought that if Hope did better than expected I would be pleased and thankful. I tried never to be discouraged by negative professionals. Doctors were always quick to show surprise after reading Hope's chart then seeing her for the first time. Once a doctor said, "From reading her chart and what she has been through, I expected to see a vegetable." While he was trying to be positive and encouraging, the word "vegetable" seemed to express a lack of respect for all life. "Vegetable" is a term loosely used to describe someone who is not only dependent on others for his daily needs, but is verbally nonresponsive. Another way the medical field defines it is "without quality of life." Even if Hope were severely physically and mentally impaired we would love her no less, and we would be proud of her will to live. She would be no less of a person, and therefore, could never be considered a vegetable no matter her level of impairment. The Bible says, "...God created man in his own image" (Genesis 1:27). God took great care in creating us; we are very special to Him, loved beyond measure. No matter what our level of function, we still have a purpose in God's sovereign plan.

I want to share with you about two very special children who could not walk, talk or feed themselves. They were dependent on others for all their needs, and yet the lives they touched will never be the same. I know because I am one of them.

Todd was born normal but contracted meningitis as a three-week old baby, and from that moment on he was never the same. Todd had severe brain damage from the infection which affected his ability to move, talk, eat, and learn. Yet there were two things Todd could still do: smile and laugh. This little boy was a great joy to be around. His smile had the power to melt your problems away. He lived to be ten years old. We visited his family after he passed away and they shared that Todd is the reason they came to know Jesus. Because of Todd's illness, his parents reached out to God. A neighbor was holding Todd when they realized something was wrong with him. The awful memory of that moment often haunted her. Through the years she observed the family and watched them grow in God's love. By their example, and through Todd's illness, they led her to Jesus. This neighbor shared her powerful testimony at Todd's funeral. We can't control illnesses and accidents, but we can trust in God with all our hearts.

Nearly 500 people attended Todd's funeral. His life had touched so many though he had no ability to speak or reach out and touch with purpose. But that didn't hinder God's love from shining through him to minister to their unmet needs. His unconditional love is a pure love from God and not many on earth are capable of giving it. There was purpose in Todd's life—to demonstrate the wonderful, unconditional love of God. I'm thankful to have known one of God's most precious gifts to mankind.

The second boy, named Brian, appeared normal at birth. Then around two years of age he was diagnosed with developmental delays. He had four older sisters and one brother. Over time his condition deteriorated until he needed total care. Many people encouraged his mother to place him in an institution. However, since the love she felt for Brian was no less than the love she shared for her other children, she sacrificed and denied her own needs to care for him. The children soon began to pitch in and help with his care. They loved him regardless of his many medical needs, which included suctioning the secretions from his lungs, daily enemas, and the time-consuming feeding process that was never ending. And though his mother, Patty, loved Brian, she was cynical about God's love. She believed God had used Brian to punish her. As our friendship grew I tried to tell her about God's amazing love for her. We lost touch over the next several years except for a few times that our paths crossed briefly. We would catch up on the latest news.

One year I ran into Patty at the mall, and she seemed changed. . . a little softer, not so bitter. She told me she had been attending church and was taking Brian with her. The rest of the children were involved in the youth group. It was there, in that church, that she had found love and acceptance. She cried when she told me, "My first Sunday visiting, the pastor came back to where I was sitting holding Brian and he took him from my arms to the front of the church and prayed for him." Weeping, she said, "No one has ever prayed for him before." Clearly God was doing a great work in her life, when, less than six months later,

Brian died at age eleven. Did his life have purpose? Absolutely! His life changed another life for eternity! Patty found meaning for her life. She found comfort knowing God loved Brian and that he was not sent for her punishment, but rather for her heart to be healed by Jesus' love and forgiveness.

~~~~

Hope has blessed our life beyond measure. I see God in her every time I look at her. I feel loved and special that God chose me to be her mom. Most things I would never have learned without Hope in my life. Hope has been teaching me patience through the years. . .to walk slower and enjoy life at every turn taking time for people along the way. She is never in a hurry no matter how I try to rush her. Hope always sees that person walking toward her and is quick to say, "Oh, hello! There you are!" It never matters to Hope who it is, a friend or a stranger, she loves them with a pure heart and makes them each feel special.

Hope often has timely and truthful words she shares, sharply cutting right to the heart of the matter. ". . . how good is a timely word" (Proverbs 15:23).

One Sunday after church Hope drove her wheelchair up to her dad. She asked, "May I have a piece of paper to write a verse on?" She wanted help jotting down Proverbs 6:10, so her dad helped her. Then she stuck it in her Bible. From there she steered her wheelchair over to a first time visitor she did not know and handed her the slip of paper. "This is for you." They began to talk and later Hope introduced me to her new friend, Alicia.

Alicia told us, "Hope gave me a verse. It's a word from God for me."

She wanted to read the verse privately. As soon as I got in the car to leave church, I pulled out my Bible and read Proverbs 6:10. "A little sleep, a little slumber, a little folding of the hands to rest—and poverty will come on you like a bandit and scarcity like an armed man." Hmm, I could only wonder if it was truly a message from God or if Hope had delivered a message that would offend a first time visitor.

That evening at our church Christmas program, Alicia came with a gift for Hope. She told us that God had rebuked her with that verse. She explained, "This morning God told me to get up out of bed three times, until finally I got out of bed and came to church."

A verse seemingly out of nowhere was exactly what Alicia needed. It was a word from God, just for Alicia, delivered by a little girl in a wheelchair, who was not too busy to listen to God.

Several years later Alicia was our waitress at a local restaurant, and we didn't recognize her, but she recognized Hope. She said, "I have never forgotten the verse you gave me. It has made a huge difference in my life."

Sometimes there are those whose eyes look at Hope and speak pity, because they can't see the world through her eyes or take joy in the little things the way she does. They may only see a burden or suffering. They don't see the "quality of life" she has and what she gives to those around her. It's unfortunate that the society in which we live looks at people and only sees their imperfections that need to be fixed. The sad reality is there are people who would choose to rid the world of those who are imperfect, because they are supposedly a burden to society. Some even sound compassionate when they justify such action by saying, "Why prolong the suffering? I wouldn't want that for my dog." But the truth is, the person who takes the time to get to know someone who has a disability may find it to be the richest, most rewarding experience of their life.

The Special Child

The child, yet unborn, spoke with the Father,

"Lord, how will I survive in the world?

I will not be like other children.

My walk may be slower,

My speech is hard to understand.

I may look different.

What is to become of me?"

The Lord replied to the child,

"My precious one, have no fear,

I will give you exceptional parents.

They will love you, because you are special,

not in spite of it.

Though your path through life will be difficult,

your reward will be greater.

You have been blessed with a special ability to

love,

and those whose lives you touch will be

blessed because you are special."

Author unknown

Taken when Hope was discharged from the hospital at 3 months old.

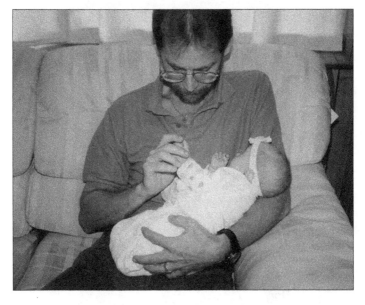

Blair holding Hope when we arrived at the adoption agency.

Hope's favorite food pasta!

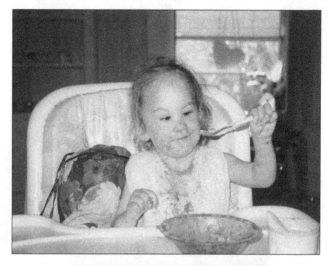

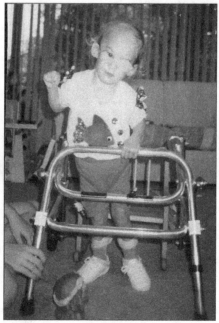

Hope standing and balancing with first walker.

Terri and Hope at 3 years old.

Hope and her Jesus pillow.

Hope in leg cast with cross bar following tendon release surgery on legs at 3 years old.

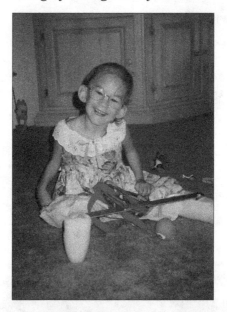

Hope in Kindergarten with first hairpiece.

Hope boating and fishing with her Mi Mi and Pa Pop.

Terri and Hope speaking at a women's conference.

Hope walking in a Care Net Walk for Life fundraiser.

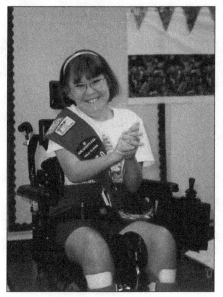

Hope in Brownies at 10 years old.

Hope received a Hero Award for National Child Health Day in 2001. Recognized by Children's Medical Services awarded by Senator Ken Pruitt. (included Terri and Nancy Gregg "Mi Mi")

Hope's first dance in middle school.

71

Hope with her birthmother and sister.

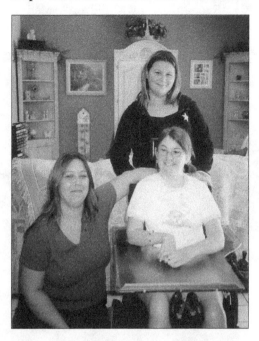

Hope with her Grandad and Granny Cartmill in Kentucky.

Hope playing wheelchair soccer at Shriners Hospital in Tampa.

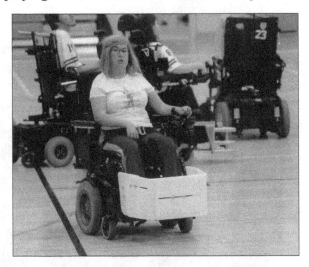

Hope swimming with the dolphins at Island Dolphin Care camp in 2007.

Stan Blair, founder of NIV Kid's Club, and
Hope met for breakfast.

Hope and her dad, Blair.

Hope and her best friend, Ashley going to Senior Prom.

Hope, dressed as Charity Church Mouse* with her
boyfriend Scott at a dance.
* (©1984 Rettino/Lkerner Publishing, www.psalty.com)

Hope in Hollywood with Selena Gomez, 2009.

Hope in Hollywood with Aly and AJ Michalka, 2009.

Hope riding a zipline at Joni and Friends Family Retreat Camp in Flatrock, NC 2010.

Hope on Homecoming Court, Senior Year.

Hope's Graduation 2010!

Hope with Vicki and Nikki, the Build-A-Bear associates at her 21st birthday party.

Hope with Don, her stepdad, at a dance.

Hope with her cousins, Logan and Jace Hovey.

Terri, Aunt Chel, Hope and Mi Mi

Hope and Butterscotch, "Kitty". She adopted Hope.

Terri and her husband, Don

Desperate Prayer

"Pray without ceasing."

~ 1Thessalonians 5:17

Recently I was at a place where time stood still. . . a place between life and death, where the knowledge of life as I knew it and felt somewhat in control was possibly coming to an end. I am not exaggerating, as God knows my heart. I was desperately crying out to God for healing of a loved one. God's word is very clear, "Confess your sins to each other and pray for each other so that you may be healed. The earnest prayer of a righteous person has great power and produces wonderful results" (James 5:16). I prayed knowing this: "And we are confident that He hears us whenever we ask for anything that pleases Him. And since we know He hears us when we make our requests, we also know that He will give us what we ask for" (1John 5:14-15). The word of God is the will of God. So I cried out to God every day for the healing of someone I loved. This was a desperate prayer, not prideful or demanding, but rather one of full surrender. God heard my cries and answered my prayer and healed my loved one.

Sometimes we do not have because we do not ask. God has answered many of Hope's prayers I thought were trivial in the scheme of life and death. However, despite my discouragement and correction, she would continue to pray without ceasing.

My mom says I always have a plan and I never give up. It is true I have an idea in my head all the time. I dreamed of meeting Aly and AJ, my favorite Disney Stars. When we got tickets to go to their concert I got my mom to go on a 'wild goose chase' to get backstage passes. My mom says I am relentless. I prayed every night that God would open the door for me to meet them backstage after the concert. And I did! When Aly and AJ saw me coming they said, "Come here, Princess." I told them something private and they really cared about what I said. I love them and I know they love me too. I had made them a lot of presents and they opened each one. We took a lot of pictures. I didn't want to leave them.

I couldn't wait to see them again. I started praying right away and kept on praying for two years. "God open the door for me to meet them again." My mom kept telling me to be thankful that

I got the meet them the first time. I was thankful, but I missed them and wanted to see them again. A friend told me about the Make-A-Wish Foundation and I applied online.

Then Make-A-Wish called me! They granted my wish to meet them again. We flew to Los Angeles and they were really excited to see me again. We spent the afternoon together, eating, talking, laughing, and trying on sunglasses. They gave me a lot of gifts too! But it was the best just being with them. They drove my wheelchair and AJ didn't do a very good job of steering. I also got to meet Selina Gomez at the same time, the paparazzi were going crazy with me and Selina!

Another Desperate Prayer Answered:

I was afraid of back surgery, too. My mom and dad didn't think I heard them talking about it while I was watching TV, but I did. I wanted to talk to Stan Blair. I only knew him from the NIV Kids' Club Christian video tapes he made. I wanted to ask him to pray for me. I prayed for Stan Blair a lot and prayed to meet him someday. I told my mom to call him, but we didn't know his number.

Hope has had her own anxieties in regards to her numerous medical conditions. One time in particular, prior to her spinal fusion and rod placement surgery, she was focused on the one thing that could help. His name was Stan Blair. Stan was the creator of NIV Kids' Club[3] whose ministry makes Bible memorization fun by putting the verses to music on CD's and DVD's. Hope's strength has been memorization through music. Through the years, God's word was planted in her heart through this man's ministry. She owns the entire collection of tapes that were originally VHS and now continues to watch them on DVD. For many of her early years, Hope was attached to Stan. Although she had never met him, she knew He was a special man of God. As she prepared for surgery, she wanted his prayers. The night before Hope's surgery she was talking to our pastor about "Stan Blair." I often had to step in and give an explanation when she spoke of him as if he were part of our family. However, this time was different because our pastor said, "I know Stan Blair."

Hope's body stiffened with excitement and I was in shock because he knew him! Hope asked, "Do you have his phone number?"

Pastor said, "Yes, as a matter of fact I do—at home." He went on to explain that Stan Blair had interviewed to be the music minister at our church a couple years earlier. In that instant, I could see God's perfect timing and how He orchestrated the situation to meet Hope's deeply felt need.

She asked, "Can you tell him to call me after my surgery?" Pastor agreed he would do that for her.

She was still groggy after anesthesia after her back surgery when she picked up the phone to hear a familiar voice, one she clearly recognized from her video tapes. She shouted, "Stan Blair, is that you?" As only He could, God met Hope's need to hear from him that day. Though the prayer was never spoken, God knew her heart's desire. Stan Blair is still a part of Hope's life 10 years later, and we have met with him twice. He recently wrote to Hope, "God used you to show me that NIV Kids' Club was really worth my time."

No prayer is insignificant to God. Even with all the small concerns, God hears them and cares more than I realized. I have learned this to be true through the answered prayers of Hope. I am in awe of Hope's faith, which motivates me to pray without ceasing in faith believing. In my entire life, I had never prayed so desperately for something as I did for the healing of my loved one. In every situation mentioned, our prayers aligned with God's will in faith and our desperate prayers were answered.

God is my provider and He is there for you 24-7 ~ Hope

~Since adopting Hope, I had prayed for her birthmother. I prayed for the day we would all meet and we could show her our love for her. ~

A Beautiful Reunion

"I thank my God upon every remembrance of you."

~ Philippians 1:3

My heart goes out to women who have placed children for adoption. I cannot imagine the feelings of loss they experience. I only know the joy and gratitude I felt because of our adoption. When someone hears Hope's story and then tells me they have placed a child for adoption my heart is filled with love and compassion for them. I know placing a child for adoption is never an easy decision. In reality, it is one of the most unselfish decisions anyone could ever make.

We had the wonderful opportunity to correspond with Hope's birthmother through the adoption agency. In the past, we sent pictures yearly with an update. We would usually hear from her birthmother once a year around the time of Hope's birthday. I am very thankful she chose to keep in touch. We have always shared with Hope the truth of her birth and adoption.

Hope's birthmother had two other children and was going through a divorce at the time of her pregnancy with Hope. After her failed abortion

God blessed Hope's birthmother with a second chance to choose life; not many women get that opportunity. We are thankful she chose life. In her letters she wrote, "I was making bad choices that were negatively affecting everyone I loved." She added that placing Hope for adoption was her chance to make a right choice for her baby. She wanted Hope to know she loved her then and always would.

One day when Hope was eleven, she came home from school and said, "Tell me about my birthmother."

I was caught off guard, as that was the first time Hope had ever directly inquired about her birthmother. I asked, "Did something happen at school?"

Hope told me, "I read a book at school today about adoption."

So we talked for a little bit and I told her, "Your birthmother wasn't able to take care of you so she gave you to us."

She said, "I thought she loved me."

I told her, "She loved you very much and she has written many letters that say so."

She wanted to see the letters. I told her when she was finished with her homework we would read them again. Once her homework was complete, we both forgot about the letters. I had started preparing dinner while we waited for her dad to come home from work. It wasn't long before Blair walked through the door that day carrying the mail. Interestingly enough, he was carrying a letter from Hope's birthmother on the very day Hope had first asked about her. The last letter we received had been a year earlier, so Hope was excited to hear from her. She could not open the letter fast enough. In a very long letter, she shared her struggles with her health and her two other children. Toward the end of the letter, Hope had lost interest, but I continued to read. Her birthmother wrote, "Please let me know if anything ever happens to our girl." I could feel the fear of the unknown in her words.

I knew it was God's will for us to open our lives to her, but I needed to consult Blair. He was not enthusiastic about this reunion. I knew he needed time to process the information. As far as he was concerned, the idea had materialized out of thin air, but in my heart I had always known the day would come. However, I truly didn't think it would be so soon. It took some time, but once Blair agreed, I quickly sent a response through the adoption agency to let the birthmother know we were open to meeting her. I knew Hope would want to meet her and if I brought up the subject she would look forward to it every day until the moment we met. Not knowing what her birthmother's response would be or when it would come, I chose not to tell Hope until we heard from her. I had always wanted Hope to have a chance to share a relationship with her biological family and it seemed the time was quickly approaching.

Some people have asked us, "Doesn't it make you angry at her for what she did to Hope?" The truth is, I have never felt anger toward Hope's birthmother. All I have ever felt for her is tremendous love and gratitude for the sacrifice she made. Hope is truly the greatest gift we have ever received.

It wasn't until one year later that we heard from her birthmother. She wrote, "I always thought I would be ready when this day came, but when it happened I was unprepared." She included her phone number in the letter and signed her name, Tonya.

When I phoned Tonya for the first time she admitted, "I'm afraid Hope will be upset with me when we meet."

I quickly reassured her, "Hope has so much love for you. She has never been angry. She will be very excited to meet you."

We continued to talk and share stories. Her birthmother was quite surprised by Hope's name. She said, "I wanted to name her Faith." She said, "Not a day goes by that I don't think of the time we shared together. I was only able to touch and hold her four times during the three months she was in the hospital."

I could hear the sense of loss in her voice; twelve years was a long time to wait to hold the child she obviously loved so dearly. By the end of the conversation she had decided to meet Hope, but she wanted to make sure Hope felt the same way.

I remember the moment my mom asked if I wanted to meet my birthmother. I could see that my mom was excited, but I didn't really understand.

Was my birthmother coming over to my house right then? At that time I was twelve years old and I had never met my birthmother, so I wasn't sure about it. I think I felt nervous to meet her. My mom gave me time to think about it, but it wasn't long before I agreed to meet her.

I called Tonya the next day and we began planning their reunion. We decided our meeting would be somewhere casual and half the distance between us. She would be bringing Hope's sister, Heather, and her biological Grandmother.

As the day of the reunion approached, everyone around us expressed apprehension and were sometimes downright negative. I had a peace because I believe God had prepared my heart for that day the moment we adopted Hope. Her biological mother was a part of her and I loved her already.

However, I could not ignore everyone's concerns and we decided to not share too much personal information initially. For example, we did not plan to tell where we lived. The day arrived and as we drove south to a quaint downtown area that had shops and restaurants, we all were a little nervous.

The day came when we went to meet my birthmother. We drove far away. I was too nervous as we drove to meet her. I usually sing in the car, but that day I was quiet. I was wondering if she would remember me.

I saw my birthmother walking toward me. She was staring at me and crying. I drove my wheelchair up to meet her and I was so excited! We hugged really tight and she remembered me! I held her and said, "I missed you." Then I asked her if she remembered me when I was in her belly for a week? She said, "I remember you every day."

As we walked to our meeting location, we saw three people approaching from the opposite direction. I was trying to make my eyes focus long distance. I thought, "Is that her birthmother? Does she look like Hope?"

It was beautiful to witness both of them hugging each other for the very first time.

I instantly felt tremendous love for this woman who gave me my precious daughter. I couldn't stifle tears that threatened, and I wept. She hugged and thanked us for taking such good care of her baby.

This reunion was touching beyond words and I wanted to shout out to everyone standing nearby, "You are witnessing a beautiful miracle—look and see our Almighty God at work!" Hope was beaming, as was everyone. It seemed as though time stood still.

Hope wasted no time after their meeting to share Jesus with her birthmother. As we all sat together under a patio table shaded by an umbrella, Hope stared at Tonya and rubbed her back.

I told her, "It's okay, I'm here. God has a plan for your life." Then I added, "Jesus loves you very much and wants to be your best friend."

Her birthmother listened and smiled while nodding her head with tears in her eyes.

We spent the entire afternoon walking around and visited over lunch. Hope wanted Tonya to sit beside her at lunch so she could hold her hand or touch her shoulder. In response, Tonya would touch Hope's hair or wipe her mouth. I realized that rather than feeling threatened, I felt proud and incredibly blessed. Proud of my daughter and the love she shared so freely. I was blessed to see God's amazing hand at work. The reunion between birthmother and daughter was as if no time had passed since the last time they met.

We went shopping and my birth grandmother bought me a Disney Monopoly game at the toy store. We ate at the Cheesecake Factory and I sat beside my birthmother and she shared her dessert with me. She actually fed me! I liked that.

Everything felt so right that something came over me at lunch and I invited them all to church the following week. Hope was scheduled to sing with a chorus. The invitation came as a surprise, as this was a deviation from the original plan. They agreed without hesitation, and would join us the following week at church and our home for lunch.

I knew it might be hard for others to comprehend, but I had that special peace that passes all understanding regarding the situation. After all, the woman was part of our family because of Hope. God was definitely in control. He was at work in the depths of Tonya's heart after finally seeing for herself that her baby had been well cared for and deeply loved. She looked as though a weight had literally been lifted from her shoulders.

The following weekend at church was beautiful. Tonya and Hope's sister, Heather, arrived at our church and met my mom and stepdad. We all sat together like one big happy family. I looked over at Tonya and the joy on her face melted my heart. She was sitting between her two daughters and holding their hands. Heather had written a letter to Hope sharing her heart about having a sister. It was very touching and is now framed on Hope's dresser. A couple of months later we shared Christmas Day with Tonya and Heather. We had a wonderful time getting to know each other better.

My birthmother, Tonya came for Christmas with my sister, Heather. They bought me a gigantic Good

Luck Bear that is green with a four leaf clover on its belly. I love Care Bears. My mom says I have hundreds but not a gigantic one like my new one! Christmas was the last time I saw my birthmother. But we are friends online and she writes to me there.

I am still in awe of how God works, preparing hearts for what the future has in store. We never know if He is preparing us for tomorrow or for twenty years from now, but either way He is trustworthy. Philippians 1:6 says, ". . . being confident of this, that he who began a good work in you will carry it on to completion until the day of Christ Jesus."

We have not seen them since that Christmas day, but they know where we are and we have a bond that time will not change—a little girl named Hope. I have prayed for Hope to have peace that passes understanding, which I know is why she seems so content with the way the relationship stands.

A Letter From Hope's Birthmother

"Look inside my life and you will know that love has etched your name on my very soul."

M.E. Miro

Although you will never remember the three short months we spent together, I relive those months every day in my mind. . . Twice I thought I would lose you forever, but you were so strong, such a fighter. Everyone admired your strength . . . Every day you were in the hospital I was there right beside you, talking to you, singing, praying. I prayed that I would be strong enough to give you the kind of family you deserved and needed. I also prayed that I could find parents to love you as much as I do, parents who could give you what I was unable to at the time of your birth. . . When you were born I knew in that instance that if I were to never make a good decision in my lifetime again, I would need to on that day. With the help of many wonderful people and I believe the Lord above who heard my prayers and knew how much I love you- Your parents came into the picture. I take comfort that you have a heaven sent family and hope one day to meet you and your family. Love always, Mommy

(Shared by permission)

The following is a poem about the love two mothers share for a child.

Legacy of an adopted child

Once there were two women who never knew each other.
One you do not remember, the other you call Mother.
Two different lives shaped to make yours one.
One became your guiding star; the other became your sun.
The first gave you life, and the second taught you to live in it.
The first gave you a need for love and the second was there to give it.
One gave you a nationality; the other gave you a name.
One gave you the seed of talent the other gave you an aim.
One gave you emotions; the other calmed your fears.
One saw your first sweet smile; the other dried your tears.
One gave you up; it was all that she could do.

The other prayed for a child and God led her straight to you.

And now you ask me through your tears,

The age old question, through the years:

Heredity or environment, which are you the product of?

Neither my darling—neither, just Two different kinds of love.

Author Unknown

I was finalizing *In That Secret Place* when God led me to ask my friend if she would consider sharing her abortion experience in our book. I knew this was God's leading because I had never considered including this before. When I asked her, she shared that God had been preparing her heart for this without her even knowing; when only days prior she was listening to a powerful sermon: "Start saying 'Yes' to God, when He opens a door for you."

Thank you, Jenn, for opening your heart and sharing your very intimate experience as God has led you in *God's Grace.*

Jenn's Story

God's Grace

"There is a way that seems right to a man,
but in the end it leads to death."

~ Proverbs 14:12

I was a 19 year old college freshman when I met my boyfriend, Pete and we were immediately smitten with one another and spent every waking moment together. Just prior to the end of my freshman year I realized I was a week late for my menstrual cycle, which was very unusual for me.

I searched the local phonebook and found a crisis pregnancy center in Tallahassee that offered free pregnancy testing. On the day before I was to return home to New Jersey for summer break, Pete and I walked into a center and were greeted by a kind woman who invited us into a small, comfortable living room with a TV. She asked questions about the nature of my visit and about my plans if my test came back positive. Overcome by fear I replied, "I don't know." I knew deep down that I would not go through with an unplanned pregnancy, but was too ashamed to admit it out loud. Before she left to do the test she asked us to watch a video. As we watched, I soon realized it explained the stages of embryonic development and I told Pete to quickly turn it off. He did, but frowned, and asked why. Feeling anxious, I began to well up with tears knowing in my heart that if I watched the video those images would captivate my heart, leaving me powerless to do what I felt I had to do: have an abortion. The woman returned shortly and said the test was negative, and I breathed a sigh of relief. We left feeling that we had narrowly escaped a tragedy.

The following month I still hadn't had a period so I went to a Planned Parenthood clinic in New Jersey for another pregnancy test, but this time the result was positive. I left the clinic in tears feeling as if abortion was my only option. Over the phone I told Pete, who was then a thousand miles away in Florida, what had happened and about my plans to have an abortion. He tried hard to talk me into keeping our baby, but I was selfishly determined to live my life according to my own plans. I wanted to finish college and "make a life for myself." I feared the humiliation an unplanned pregnancy would bring and the reactions of my parents, family and friends. I mistakenly thought having an abortion would allow me to resume life as I'd previously known it.

Desperate to get my life back to normal I rejected the truth that there was a developing baby inside of me. In May of 1992 I chose to end my child's life alone and in secrecy. I foolishly believed I was resolving a problem. Little did I realize that I had caused the greatest harm I would ever know.

As time passed I often thought about our child. I calculated the approximate date of its birth and sadly realized it would have been born around Christmas (near my birthday and also my favorite time of year). Occasionally, I calculated the baby's age and wondered whether it would've been a boy or a girl. I wondered what I would have named it and what it would have looked like.

In the five years following my abortion I did exactly as I had planned, living life on my terms. I made a pact with myself to "do something with my life." Perhaps I could make up for my heinous act by accomplishing my dreams and contributing to the world in a positive way. I graduated from college in 1995 and married Pete in 1997. And even though life was going according to my plan, the memory of my child haunted me continually. I became increasingly aware that my abortion had left a gaping hole inside of me. I tried to forget what I had done, but my mind and heart wouldn't let go. I was bound in a prison of my own making, ashamed and guilt-ridden. I knew deep inside that I had sinned against God by killing the life He created inside of me. His forgiveness was all that mattered to me because my sin was against Him.

Although I had been raised Christian I had a shallow understanding of the forgiveness available to me through Jesus' death on the cross. Five years after my abortion, I found the forgiveness I yearned for through Jesus when I learned that "if we confess our sins to Him, he is faithful and just to forgive us and to cleanse us from every wrong" (1 John 1:9). So I confessed my sins and since that day I have found He is faithful to His promises. The Bible says: "Therefore, if anyone *is* in Christ, *he is* a new creation; old things have passed away; behold, all things have become new" (2Corinthians 5:17). I found Jesus along with His compassion, mercy and forgiveness for my abortion and He has changed my life forever.

God's Word says that, ". . . to all who mourn, he will give beauty for ashes, joy instead of mourning, praise instead of despair. . ." (Isaiah 61:3). "He heals the brokenhearted, binding up their wounds" (Psalm 147:3) and "The LORD is close to the brokenhearted; he rescues those who are crushed in spirit" (Psalm 34:18). I can testify to the truth of these scriptures for He rescued me and I now have joy in place of mourning.

~~~

"For it is by *grace* you have been saved, through faith–and this not from yourselves, it is the gift of God–not by works, so that no one can boast." ~ Ephesians 2:8-9

During this journey of healing, I became friends with a woman named Hope—one of only a few people I shared my abortion story with. One night she asked if I had ever named my aborted baby. I said I had not and she said it would be a good idea. She asked, "So, what would you like to name it? Do you think it was a boy or a girl?" I had no answers. I realized how precious God's forgiveness is—how "Grace" is the undeserved favor He showed toward me. And I knew the baby's name was Grace. I smiled through tears as I said the baby's name should be Grace. Until that moment I had never allowed myself to grieve her loss, but naming her finally gave her the dignity she deserved. Hope prayed with me, thanking God for His forgiveness and for Grace, and that night I released my baby into God's care once and for all. I am comforted by the knowledge that she is in heaven and that there is no better place for her.

Since then, God has shown me even more *grace* by allowing me to have three more children with my husband Pete. I find myself, even to this day, looking at photos of all three of my children together and saying in the quietness of my heart, "There's one missing." It is evidence that Grace will never be forgotten. She has a permanent place all her own in my heart and in our family.

Why is she growing?
If she is not a human being. . .
What kind of being is she?
If she is not a child. . .
Why is she sucking her thumb?
If she is a living, human child. . .
Why is it legal to kill her?
Author Unknown

Fetal Development

At Conception:

Day 1 The sperm from the father penetrates the mother's egg cell.

The DNA on a single human cell contains enough information to fill an entire set of the Encyclopedia Britannica (30 volumes).[4]

Day 18-20 Spinal cord, brain and nervous system foundations begin to develop.

Day 21 Heartbeat begins.

Day 28-32 Face makes first appearance with mouth, tongue and nose beginning to take shape.

Day 40 Baby making first reflex movement.

Day 44 Electrical activity in brain noted.

Day 52 Spontaneous movement begins.

8 weeks Baby's body is well-proportioned. Every organ is present and beginning to function.

8 ½ weeks Baby can feel pain. [5]

9 weeks "Baby is well enough formed to bend his fingers round an object in the palm of his hand. In response to a touch on the sole of his foot he will curl his toes or bend his hips and knees to move away from the touching object."[6]

10 weeks Fingerprints and fingernails begin to form.

11 weeks Baby can make facial expressions.

13 weeks Baby is active within the womb.

4 months Baby turns somersaults. Sleep patterns are developing.

5 months Mother may feel baby kick.

6 months Baby stretches when she wakes from sleeping.

7 months Opening of eyelids occur.

8 months Living quarters is cramped for baby.

9 months Baby triggers labor and soon makes grand entrance into the world.

The Most Dangerous Place in the World

"You intended to harm me, but God intended it for good to accomplish what is now being done, the saving of many lives."

~ Genesis 50:20

I cannot write a book about Hope without mentioning the issue of abortion. Abortion is not something people like to hear about, but our family lives with the reality of abortion every day. Hope had been growing in the womb of her mother for ten and a half weeks when her mother went to have an abortion. At that time, Hope was already completely and perfectly formed. Her heart had been beating since approximately day 21 and by eight weeks she was well-proportioned, about the size of a thumb. Every organ was present. By the 10th week her fingerprints and fingernails were beginning to form.[7] It was at this stage of development when the abortionist's curette, a loop-shaped steel knife entered the womb. The instrument was meant to end Hope's life, yet miraculously she escaped. Hope was alive, but not without harm. The instrument cut a large section of her scalp and skull leaving her brain exposed.

Abortion is performed in secret, but Hope's scar is clear evidence that cannot be denied.

Every day we realize how close she came to death. We see the scar on Hope's head as a reminder that God spared her life among the 54,559,615 babies that have been aborted since 1973 when Roe v. Wade was passed in the United States.[8] With that decision, the United States Supreme Court declared it unconstitutional for individual state laws to protect unborn children from abortion. The protective hand of a government that previously outlawed abortion was now removed.

Now abortion is legal throughout all nine months of pregnancy. While propaganda may say otherwise statistics state:

- 1% of all abortions occur because of rape or incest;
- 6% of abortions occur because of potential health problems regarding either the mother or child
- 93% of all abortions occur for social reasons (i.e. the child is unwanted or inconvenient).[9]

The "mother's health" is a very vague term that is used to justify abortion for any reason. It leaves the definition wide open to interpretation, which translates as abortion on demand. National statistics from 1995-2004, reveal an average of one out of every four pregnancies was terminated by abortion.[10] And though people toss in a wide variety of excuses for why it is necessary to end the life of another, statistics reveal it is primarily a social decision.

Many believe abortion should be available for those who do not want to have a disabled child. Medical researchers estimate that 80% or more of babies now prenatally diagnosed with Down's Syndrome are aborted.[11]

Adoption is often not even deemed an option, as I have heard people say, "I could never place my child for adoption." Adoption might be a harder, more painful decision, but abortion ends a life and that is reality. The baby in the womb is not just a living being when the mother wants her baby. The circumstances surrounding a pregnancy do not change the fact that a live human being is growing within the womb.

I have also heard the argument; abortion decreases the chances of an unwanted child being abused. The fact remains; abortion is truly the ultimate child abuse. Since abortion is performed in secret, we can't hear the screams or see the tears or feel the agonizing pain, so denial is easier.

Science has proven the baby begins to move at about 7 ½ weeks after conception. Developmental facts are widely published from medical references and easily found on the internet. Dr. Steven Zielinski testified before Congress that an unborn child could feel pain at "eight-and-a-half weeks and possibly earlier".[12] "Nine weeks after conception the baby is well enough formed to bend his fingers round an object in the palm of his hand. In response to a touch on the sole of his foot he will curl his toes or bend his hips and knees to move away from the touching object."[13] On an ultrasound you can clearly see the baby touch his face and suck his thumb. There is also a video called *The Silent Scream*, which is the video recording of a first trimester baby during an abortion. The baby is moving away from the instrument intended to take its life. Video may be viewed at: www.silentscream.org.[14]

We are rarely exposed to the stacks of murdered infant corpses, unless we seek the truth, which is often quite well hidden from public view. But for true seekers the truth is very easy to find, if they will just search the Internet. But be warned; the truth is very painful and hard to handle. The Center for Bio-Ethical Reform has a video at www.abortionno.org. [15] Many people would prefer to ignore what is happening in secret, and pass it off as merely a women's rights issue.

Underneath the hidden agenda and rhetoric, a baby is being murdered. His life is purposely being ended. And whether the pro-abortion side admits it or not, it is a moral issue. Denial is less painful, but truth, according to Scripture, will actually set the captives free. Seek truth for yourself.

Being Hope's mother has opened many opportunities to share the truth about abortion and fetal development. Hope and I have shared her story with many high school classes and churches over the years. The reaction is always one of shock and disbelief. One would think high school students would be more informed about abortion. Every time I am shocked to learn how little they really know and how misinformed they are. One high school senior told her teacher after we spoke,

"This was the best class I have ever had!" Later that day her mother called the school adminis-trator complaining about our subject matter.

Give Me the Microphone, Please

Every year my mom and I go to speak at a high school for Disability Awareness Week. We have done it many times. Now that I am an adult I do most of the talking and the kids really listen to me. My mom tells the story about my birth, then I take over. I have a plan of course! I usually tell them about myself and answer their questions. I ask them questions too. They are surprised when I remember their names and call on them. In one class there was a boy named Raphael (that is one of the Ninja Turtle names) who left the room when I was speaking. I noticed he was gone a long time. I asked the teacher "Where is Raphael?" Everyone knew he was gone and then when he came back everyone teased him. I asked him, "What took you so long? I missed you." This class was all boys in 11th grade. We had a dance off. They danced with me to Miley Cyrus' Hoe Down Throw Down song. One boy did the worm dance on the floor. I think he won. Raphael did not dance, I think he was shy. At the end of the class, I asked Raphael to pray for me and he prayed out loud. He gave me his phone number and I used to call him and we would talk; he was just a friend. I have made a lot of friends by sharing about being handicapped.

Abortion is simply a word to which many have become desensitized, but after hearing Hope's story, the truth is often more difficult to ignore or deny.

Even the message of fetal development is met with surprise with educated adult individuals. Recently I was talking to a nurse who thought a seven week gestational miscarriage is not really a formed baby! I told her to look pictures up on the Internet which she quickly did to prove me wrong and was surprised to see arms, legs and a baby's face.

I served on the Board at a local pregnancy center and opportunities were made available for Hope and I to share in different venues. We spoke at an abstinence rally. Several years later, a teenage boy walked up to us in the community and told Hope he had heard her story at the rally and because of her he was pro-life.

While on the board during my first term, I organized a twenty-four hour Help Line. The first time my phone rang on the Help Line the caller asked, "How much are your abortions?"

My heart skipped a beat. While I paused for a deep breath, I realized that she was mistakenly calling, thinking we offered abortions. I informed the caller, "We do not provide or refer for abortion." Then I asked the caller, "Are you sure you're pregnant?"

She said, "Yes, I am sure. I'm about eight weeks and I want an abortion, because I get so sick and I don't have a job."

I told her, "Your baby's heart was beating since she was twenty-one days old and she has had brain wave activity since she was forty-four days old."[16] I further explained, "By eight weeks all your baby's organs were formed and your baby is moving inside even though you cannot feel it."

She was adamant in her decision to abort and did not want to make an appointment to discuss other viable options. She continued to share that she had two other kids and was in the middle of a separation. I silently prayed *Help me, Lord.* I shared with her how my daughter had survived an abortion. Before the conversation ended, I prayed with the caller regarding her morning sickness. But she was quick to hang up without making an appointment. I felt discouraged when I hung up the phone, believing she would choose abortion, and that I would never know the end of her story.

One night, seven months later, I was volunteering on the helpline again. I asked God to *show me if this is what He wanted me to do.* I wanted to see more of what God was doing in the lives of the women with unplanned pregnancies. I wanted to do more. Later that evening, I received a call from a mother who was concerned because she had postpartum depression. As a nurse I understood this hormone change, but I explained I couldn't relate to what she was going through because I had adopted.

The caller stopped me in the middle of my sentence and said, "I think I talked to you when I called before. I was going to have an abortion and you told me about your daughter." Even as she spoke her voice seemed to lighten and I could hear happiness as she said, "After we hung up from talking, I called my friend who was also pregnant and scheduled for an abortion. We both decided then to have our babies. I was not sick another day after you prayed for me."

I was overcome with joy as I realized God was specifically showing me I was in His will, doing what He called me to do. He had answered my prayer for healing this dear woman and that Hope's testimony had changed the course of history for these two babies and their mothers. The abortionist intended to harm Hope by taking her life, but God intended it for good when He spared her.

Another very memorable call I received was from a very angry young man. He wanted his girlfriend to have an abortion. I explained we weren't a medical facility and asked, "Are you sure she is pregnant?" I encouraged him to bring her for counseling.

He seemed mad at the world as he shouted, "There is no way she is having this baby because her mom is retarded and I don't want a retarded baby too!" I suggested adoption as another option. "There is no way anyone would want this baby!" He went on to explain he had epilepsy and asthma which ran in both of their families. He believed no one would want a child like this because he didn't want that responsibility either. God opened the door for me to share Hope's story.

I asked him if I could tell him about my daughter and he agreed. I explained to him, "My daughter Hope has all those disabilities you are afraid your unborn child will have and we adopted her. I couldn't imagine loving her anymore." I explained that I was a nurse and I know he is afraid, but there is no way to guarantee that his child would have all those disabilities. He was not pleased at all with Hope's testimony. He wanted an escape, not someone to side with the baby. He wanted someone to justify his reasons to end this baby's life. He wasn't at peace with his decision; he was filled with anger because this was out of his control. This wasn't planned and he didn't want it. I don't know what ever happened to that little child. Was the baby born with all the anomalies he imagined? I would suspect not if the baby was even given the chance to live. I am reminded of the verse: *"Speak up for those who cannot speak for themselves, for the right of all who are destitute" (Proverbs 31:8).*

This issue involves so much more than mere "choice." The truth is that abortion destroys the life of a baby and leaves the woman emotionally wounded.

I have talked to many women who have chosen abortion, many of whom were never encouraged to keep the baby or place it for adoption. Most women I have talked to would not have chosen abortion if they had felt there was any encouragement or any other viable option. In retrospect, they would have chosen life for their babies. They all shared feelings of remorse, guilt and sadness realizing abortion killed their child. One friend, a pastor's wife, referred to herself as a "murderer." Day in and day out those who have had abortions live with the horror, haunted by their choices. There is no way to undo the past and the guilt nearly always weighs heavily on their souls.

A special prayer by Hope, April 2001

"Just praise the Lord, I said just praise the Lord, when your heart is broken in two just praise the Lord. I said just praise the Lord. Don't worry or be scared. Just praise the Lord. I said just praise the

Lord. When you manage to do wrong. Don't worry. Just praise the Lord. Ask Jesus to come and live in your heart and Praise the Lord."

Many suffer from Post-Abortion Syndrome, which is similar to Post-Traumatic Stress Syndrome. There are many symptoms for this condition. A partial list includes: guilt, anxiety, psychological numbing, depression and thoughts of suicide, eating disorders, drug and alcohol abuse, and survival guilt.[17] Some women believe they have committed the unforgivable sin by having an abortion, but that is not the truth. The truth is that God loves these dear women more than they can even imagine. He sent His son Jesus to die to redeem them from their sins. Aside from God's grace and tender mercy none of us is worthy of forgiveness, but He gives it freely and unconditionally to all who ask. If you are desperate to feel forgiven after an abortion, just accept God's forgiveness and know that ". . . as far as the east is from the west, so far does he remove our sins from us" (Psalm 103:12).

Many of the men and women who sit in church have experienced abortion. Many are frightened to share the pain they hide inside. I believe with all my heart, abortion will end when the silence is finally broken; when the cries of the numerous women who have suffered from abortions are heard openly throughout the world-not just in secret. I realize this is a very sensitive issue and many wounds run deep. However, it is important to realize that God can turn pain into joy. He can make good out of bad when you entrust your life into His hands. Something Satan meant for evil …to destroy you, God wants to use for His glory. He wants to proclaim truth to others of His transforming healing power.

If you haven't experienced God's love and forgiveness from your abortion, I want you to know there is help available. Contact a Pregnancy Center near you at www.optionline.org[18] or online there is post-abortion support.[19]

"And I am convinced that nothing can ever separate us from God's love. Neither death nor life, neither angels nor demons, neither our fears for today nor our worries about tomorrow—not even the powers of hell can separate us from God's love. No power in the sky above or in the earth below—indeed, nothing in all creation will ever be able to separate us from the love of God that is revealed in Christ Jesus our Lord" (Romans 8:38-39).

God created us individually and has a plan for each of our lives no matter our ability or disability. There is no life that is insignificant to God. From the moment of conception until our natural death, we are valuable to Him. He knows the number of hairs on our head and keeps our tears in a jar. God's unconditional love and forgiveness for us is fierce and has no end.

Everyone tells me I am a miracle and that I am special, but I don't feel any more special than anyone else. I know my birthmother had an abortion that didn't work and I survived. I know abortion kills babies. I don't want to know any more about abortion than I already know because it is a very bad thing. My birthmother wrote and said she feels guilty. I asked my mom, "Why does she feel guilty?" My mom told me it was because she had an abortion and I am handicapped. I told my mom, "Tell her I forgive her and I love her."

A Note for the Reader

I pray for those who read *In That Secret Place* just as I prayed during the writing of this book. My prayer to God over this entire book has been:

Inspire Me

May my heart be opened by Your touch.

May my words be spoken with love.

May my intent be to give You glory.

May my eyes see the world as You do.

May You impart wisdom as I seek to share.

May Your truth be spread as seed upon a fertile ground.

May I love freely with all my heart.

May my desire always be to be Your vessel.

By Terri Kellogg

The writing process has been an enjoyable experience for me. My favorite time to write was in the fall with the windows open with a warm cup of cappuccino beside me. Although I was never especially interested in writing a book, one day I began and simply never stopped. I felt strongly that God wanted me to share Hope's story. I've worked on this project for over fifteen years. It has changed through the years as I have changed and grown. Everything I shared is true and straight from my heart.

I pray the message is simple and straightfor-wardly pointing to Jesus, the One who has been our strength. Though none of us are perfect, God loves us just as we are and wants us to follow Him. If you have never believed in His Son Jesus Christ for your salvation ". . . today is the day of salvation" (2 Corinthians 6:2). No one knows what tomorrow may bring, but the Bible tells us there is only one way to God. Jesus answered, "I am the way and the truth and the life. No one comes to the Father except through me" (John 14:6). "I have come that they may have life, and have it to the full" (John 10:10). "Look around you, not at your circumstances, but at creation. For since the creation of the world God's invisible qualities- his eternal power and divine nature- have been clearly seen, being understood from what has been made, so that men are without excuse" (Romans 1:20).

God has promised, "You will seek me and find me when you seek me with all your heart" (Jeremiah 29:13).

I have only done what God has called me to do. I pray that Hope's story has blessed and encouraged you. Please feel free to share it with others. We would love to hear from you! If our story has impacted your life or if you would like to share your story with us, please see our contact information at the end.

Jan 8, 2001

After reading Psalms 8 together one night, Hope wrote and sang this song.

"Oh Lord, Oh Lord, what can I do to live my life for you?

Oh Lord, Oh Lord what can I do? What can I do for you?

Oh Lord, Oh Lord come into my heart, come into my heart to live.

Oh Lord, Oh Lord I want to live my life for you.

Oh Lord, Oh Lord I want to share the good news.

To tell them you love them.

Oh Lord, Oh Lord I love you.

I love you with all my heart.

Oh Lord, Oh Lord I praise your name.

I will praise your name and clap my hands."

I hope you loved reading **In That Secret Place** that we put together for you. Since you know me now you can call me by my nickname, Hopey!

The End

Hope Hoffman

Where We Are Now

We all experienced a gigantic milestone. . . Hope's graduation from High School, the Class of 2010. She was one of over 400 graduates. The school had rented a portable wheelchair lift to raise her to the level of the stage. Her dad, Aunt, grandparents, cousins, and I were in awe as we watched Hope drive across the stage with a huge smile on her face as over 3,000 people gave her a standing ovation for the entire two minutes it took to enter and exit the stage. The miracle here was that the air horns blaring in the background never gave her as much as a twitch. She has come so far, and in that moment I realized she is grown up now. As a graduate Hope is in job training through the off campus program through the school system. Hope does have some entrepreneurial ideas and I am excited to see what God is going to do in her future. I am trusting God with her today, tomorrow and the future. He has shown me that He is more than capable.

Hope's first project was helping contribute her feelings and ideas to *In That Secret Place.* Many times she had other activities that were more interesting however, I was occasionally able to persuade her. One afternoon while working on the book I said to Hope, "I really need you to help me out here."

She said with a chuckle, "Okay, that will be $10." She continued eating her lunch knowing I was watching her. She looked up with a grin, "I know. . . I drive a hard bargain."

Within the twenty-one years of Hope's journey, among our difficulties, divorce struck home, which is never easy and hard to accept. It is not something I ever dreamed would happen to me and that failure is a disappointment. Since the divorce I have come to grasp the truth of God's love for me and it is not based on my goodness. I am a child of God, forgiven and loved. The truth is that simple and I know it firsthand.

Our God is a God of second chances and His love for us never changes. I have remarried a man who loves Jesus and lives his life humbly. He has loved Hope as his very own. If I had been looking I could have never found him and I know he is a gift from God. Hope easily received her stepdad into her heart. They share a love of pasta together as they are both Italian. He has brought her biological roots alive and the bond they share is very special.

Hope and her dad continue to spend much time together and she will always be Daddy's little girl.

My Dreams

I do want to get married when I am 24 years old. I want to marry someone I can really talk to, with cute looks, matching hair and a great personality! I'm not worried about the future, because I will always have a plan and if my plan doesn't work God's plan will be better my mom tells me.

~Terri and Hope would love to speak to your women's group, fundraiser banquet, high school, or church group on any one of several subjects including abortion, adoption, disability, or caregiving. For more information visit our website at www.inthatsecretplace.com or email us at hopeandterri@inthatsecretplace.com~

Endnotes

[1] W.E. Vine, M.A., ,Vine's Expository Dictionary of New Testament Words, Macdonald Publishing Company, "hope," pg 572.

[2] Rachael K. Jones, Mira R.S. Zolna, Stanley K. Henshaw and Lawrence B. Finer, "Abortion in the United States: Incidence and Access to Services, 2005," Perspectives on Sexual and Reproductive Health, Vol. 40, Number1, March 2008, pg 6, <htpp://www.guttmacher.org/pubs/journals/4000608.pdf>, (June 28, 2010).

[3] NIV Kids Club, Blair Music, Content Copyright 2009-2010, July 3, 2010 <http://www.nivkid-sclub.com>, (July 3, 2010).

[4] Creation Wiki Encyclopedia of Creation Science, <http://www.creationwiki.org/cloning>, (June 20, 2010).

[5] Steven Ertelt, Editor, New Study Denying Fetal Pain Lacks Scientific Basis Pro-Life Groups Say, LifeNews.com, June 28, 2010,< http://www.lifenews.com/int1580.html>, (July 11, 2010).

[6] H.B. Valman and J.F. Pearson. "What the Foetus Feels", *British Medical Journal,* January 26, 1980, quoted in "Human development from conception to birth", Society for the Protection of Unborn Children, 2010, <http://www.spuc.org.uk/ethics/abortion/human-development>, (July 11, 2010).

[7] Michael Monahan, Heritage House '76, Inc, Milestones of Early Life, Copyright 2006, <http://abortionfacts.com/literature/literature 9438ms.asp>, (July 11, 2010).

[8] National Right to Life Committee, 2010, "U.S. Abortion Statistics by Year (1973-current)," *National Right to Life Factsheet,* January 2010, Christian Life Resources, Inc. Updated January 2010,<http://www.Christianliferesources.com/?5511 >, (July 1, 2010).

[9] The Center for Bio-Ethical Reform, "Abortion Facts," Copyright 1996-2008, <http://www.abortionno.org/index.php/abortion facts/> June 20, 2010, The Alan Guttmacher Institute, <htpp://www.agi-usa.org>, (June 20, 2010).

[10] Ventura SJ, Abma JC, Mosher WD, Henshaw SK. Estimated pregnancy rates by outcome for the United States, 1990–2004. National vital statistics reports; vol 56 no 15, pg 13, Hyattsville, MD: National Center for Health Statistics. 2008, <http://www.cdc.gov/nchs/data/nvsr/nvsr56/nvsr56_15.pdf >, (April 14, 2008).

[11] George Neumayr, "The New Eugenics," The American Spectator, (July 13, 2005), <http://www.orthodoxytoday.org/articles5/NeumayrNewEugenics.php>, (July 3, 2010).

[12] Steven Ertelt, Editor, New Study Denying Fetal Pain Lacks Scientific Basis Pro-Life Groups Say, LifeNews.com, June 28, 2010,< http://www.lifenews.com/int1580.html>, (July 11, 2010).

[13] H.B. Valman and J.F. Pearson. "What the Foetus Feels", *British Medical Journal,* January 26, 1980, quoted in "Human development from conception to birth", Society for the Protection of Unborn Children, 2010, <http://www.spuc.org.uk/ethics/abortion/human-development>, (July 11, 2010).

[14] The Silent Scream, <http://www.silentscream.org/video/SScream%20English/SilentSc_Eng_3.mov>, site updated April 2007, Copyright 1998-2207 by Several Sources Shelters, (July 7, 2010).

[15] The Center for Bio-Ethical Reform, Graphically Exposing the Injustice of Abortion, <http://www.AbortionNO.org>, (July 7, 2010).

[16] O'Rahilly, R. and Muller, F., Human Embryology and Teratology, 3rd Edition, New York: John Wiley and Sons, Inc., 2001, taken from Michael Monahan, Heritage House '76, Inc, Milestones of Early Life, Copyright 2006, <http://abortionfacts.com/literature/literature_9438ms.asp>, (July 11, 2010).

[17] Sidna Masse, "Post Abortion Sundrome Symptoms", Ramah International, <http://rama-hinternational.org/post-abortion-syndrome-symptoms.html >, (July 11,2010).

[18] Pregnant? You need help? You have options: 1-800-395-help, <http://optionline.org>, (July11,2010).

[19] Safe Haven, A Place for Healing from the Trauma of Abortion, copyright 2007-2009 by SafeHavenMinistries.com, <http://www.postabor-tionpain.com>, (July 11, 2010).

CPSIA information can be obtained
at www.ICGtesting.com
Printed in the USA
BVHW070031200122
626587BV00001B/106